A LATER DAY, ANOTHER YEAR

Other books of poetry by
ERNEST SANDEEN

Collected Poems, 1953–1977
Like Any Road Anywhere
Children and Older Strangers
Antennas of Silence

A LATER DAY, ANOTHER YEAR
Poems, 1977–1988

Ernest Sandeen

Ernest Sandeen

Inscribed for Bill and Ursula
Notre Dame
Oct. 5, 1991

UNIVERSITY OF NOTRE DAME PRESS
NOTRE DAME, INDIANA

Copyright © 1989 by
University of Notre Dame Press
Notre Dame, Indiana 46556
All Rights Reserved

Manufactured in the United States of America

Library of Congress Cataloging-in-Publication Data

Sandeen, Ernest Emanuel, 1908–
  A later day, another year.

  I. Title.
PS3537.A6233L3 1989   811'.52   88-33886
ISBN 0-268-01288-1

In Memory of My Parents,
Mabel and Will

Contents

PREFACE	xiii
ENTRANCES HAUNTED BY EXITS	1
Dialogue at the Door	3
New Acquaintance	4
Prayer for a Seemly Stance	5
Seventy-Fourth Birthday	6
At the Kitchen Sink	7
How Time Is Kept	8
Old Man Looking Ahead	9
Journey through the Cloud of Unknowing	10
What His Nurse Heard	11
To Get the Most out of a Hanging	12
Neo-Scholasticism, 1980's	13
A Journey of the Mental Traveler	14
For Men Only	15
The Prowler	16
In Bed Alone	17
My Two Lives	18
The Son of Man	19
A High-Toned Old Christian Gentleman	20
Genesis 7:27	21
The Night after Sleep	22

viii   Contents

GAMES NOT TO BE TOYED WITH   23

Behind Home Plate   25
At Center Court   26
By Firefly to Tokyo and Back   27
Translating the Latin   28
Evidence   30
Metaporn   31
Solitaire Lotto   32

NATURAL RELATIONS   33

Gardening through the Ages   35
Smell of Survival, Long Range   37
Birds, Chimneys   38
Winter Holiday in Sunshine City   39
Mid-Winter Greetings   40
Mountain   41
Interrogation   42
Quandary   44
The Twister that Missed Us   45
Incident in a Rain of Violence   46
Astronomy   47
A Late Twentieth-Century Prayer   48

FAMILY RELATIONS   49

Tricycle   51
Incident in a Long Story   53
Watching the Nightly TV News   54
Recent Family History   55
Love Song in a Minor Key   56
Eileen and the Daylilies   57
Her Wealth of Shells   58
For Eileen on Her Birthday   60
Daughter Departing, Arriving   63
What Can "Grand" Mean?   65

Contents ix

FELLOW TRAVELERS 67

Time and Again 69
Resistance 70
Oldest Guest at the Celebration 71
Injunction to the Young 72
Gerontocrats 73

Acknowledgments

The author makes grateful acknowledgment to the following publications in which these poems first appeared:

Cedar Rock
    "By Firefly to Tokyo and Back," Fall 1984
Konglomerati Press
    "Winter Holiday in Sunshine City," December 4, 1982
Michigan Quarterly Review
    "At Center Court," Fall 1982
The New Republic
    "Smell of Survival, Long Range," July 4 & 11, 1981
    "Tricycle," September 6, 1982
PN Review
    "Gardening through the Ages," 1981
    "Old Man Looking Ahead," 1981
    "For Eileen on Her Birthday: Walking with Her around Saint Joseph's Lake," 1984
Poetry
    "How Time Is Kept," August 1978
    "Interrogation," January 1984
    "Seventy-Fourth Birthday," January 1984
    "Translating the Latin," January 1984
    "A Journey of the Mental Traveler," December 1986
    "Dialogue at the Door," December 1986
    "The Prowler," December 1986
    "My Two Lives," December 1986
    "A Late Twentieth-Century Prayer," October–November 1987

Poetry Northwest
    "Birds, Chimneys," Autumn 1982
The Wallace Stevens Journal
    "Quandary," Spring 1985
    "A High-Toned Old Christian Gentleman," Spring 1985

Preface

Your late years are the grace period given you by luck or circumstance in which to retrieve your earlier life, though its final meaning may still elude you. It is then that you discover how you have relived your childhood and youth, again and again, in various disguises adjusted to the changes of human and solar time beyond your control.

Entrances Haunted by Exits

Dialogue at the Door

I had no intention
of coming this way again,
but here I am. Do you
still have light for me?

Yes, but not as bright as before.

And the darkness?

Not as deep and dense.
Expect sleep to be
foreshortened, dreams more shallow.

Has this place become
more narrow, then, than it was?

No; in fact, much wider,
but air is thinner.
Muscles of mind and body
have to breathe harder.

Well, then, shall I come back in,
as if beginning once more?

Dear old friend, it's not
your choice. You must.

New Acquaintance

At the bottom of the stairs
I glimpse my body, for the first time,
as an outmoded model of me.

Surprised, the most I can promise is
that up there in my bedroom I'll undress
him, fit him into baggy pajamas,

roll him into my bed and fold him
into my sleep where we can dream
memories together or not dream at all.

Prayer for a Seemly Stance

It means help me now not to stoop
with the retrograde inclination of joints
and bones and consenting muscles
toward the postures of old men which my limber
youth could enact precisely on the college
theater stage but could not foretell.

Seventy-Fourth Birthday

What is new? I've been mortal all
my life. It's only that now I suspect
where I have lived is where I live.
Ancestors are many layers deep,
too deep, too many for me to count.

A voice in the cool of evening searches
through a faulted garden. It nags
at the eroding gravestones: "What
was your crime?" "We were for many years
alive but at last got caught."

AT THE KITCHEN SINK

After the last dinner dish
is rinsed and dried,
the faucet, turned off,
continues to drip.
It should not be allowed
to tick away the seconds
of something as precious
as a lifetime. Yet it does,
it does, it does.

How Time Is Kept

In the flurry of our beating hearts
there is never time enough for what we dream of.
Our intimate dead, however, lie calm of face
as if to say, no need for hurry.
They idle in such a wealth of stillness
it can never be wholly spent.

Yet they are close, deep in our one affair.
Don't disturb us, they say, we are busy
at the leisure of not breathing. It takes all
our time, it takes more time than being alive.

Old Man Looking Ahead

Maybe it's only one final fact,
much smaller than you expected,
which then will slip into place, to complete,
not the answer, but the question.

And you with your coronet of darkness
to make you invisible, your wallet
stuffed with the relics of your own bones,
given that responsible grace

of keeping fresh the uncreated
stillness, not even needing
to know that without you
the silence would be imperfect.

Journey through the Cloud of Unknowing

This morning in his seventy-ninth year our friend
proved his mortality and so became earthly whole,
leaving us behind, not yet complete, able

only to imagine his flight on an instant wavelength,
neither up nor down, and no longer outbound but inbound,
back to the first impulse, and there to undergo,

together with all his galaxies, an implosive
annihilation; and in the first blink of extinction
to discover that during the eons made of swirling,

exploded fragments, his true place, from the start,
reposed intact in the unbroken body of nothingness.
How could he have dared to foresee it? to be drawn

unerringly into a total idleness as innocent
of every wisp of created being as it was before
the beginning, nothing but glory now, and he

completely himself, transfigured into praise,
all his words outgrown, his grammar obsolete.

What His Nurse Heard

Minutes before his death
he said
I'm glad
I had good teeth

To Get the Most out of a Hanging

This stairway leading you up was not
constructed for your coming down.
The few makeshift steps you climb

were meant to dwarf whatever height
you may at times have dreamed of. When you're
manacled, hooded, and the false floor

caves in, it's arranged that your own weight
will jerk the rope strangle-taut, giving
your love of life the abrupt look of a suicide.

Neo-Scholasticism, 1980's

How many viral demons
can dance on the point
of a needle, or the tip
of a penis?

A Journey of the Mental Traveler

Resurrection from a body where I had spent
my life proved harder and took longer than expected.
The scalpel-spear all but bled me away
into my sac of urine swollen, drop by drop,
as from a leaking ocean. Diminished to an impulse,
I had to swim, holding my breath, through sea-salt
miles of arteries and veins until a limp heart
surrendered me to lungs slowly forgetting how to breathe.

But here was air, it lifted me tall enough
for brain to open ears and eyes, rouse naked
intimacies of touch. Tongue was loosened
to answer the sound of my pseudonym by which
I could recognize myself though as yet unnamed.

Yet parts of me have been left behind
in obscure nooks of cells and organs.
People and things have grown so compactly real,
so intensely present, they caricature the wide
echoing estates of time and space I afforded them
when I was living, I thought, the true story of myself.

I search such sleep as I am given
for a dream of quiet talk with Mary
and Martha in their garden. They, endowed
with wombs, should know better than he, how well
their brother managed a second life, a second death.

For Men Only

The lab report: "Well differentiated
Adenocarcinoma, Gleason Grade iii/x."
Both doctors (M.D.) agree that nothing
needs to be done, that there's nothing
to worry about, that these atypical
cells, though mad, typically sleep
where they are, like Rip Van Winkle,
for twenty years or so.

Still, "Adenocarcinoma" does not
translate well in the dictionary:
"A malignant tumor originating
in glandular tissue"—for example,
the prostate, for example, yours.

The doctors find especially
good news in "Well differentiated"
and in "Gleason Grade iii/x."
And what can you do but nod
your head in profound sympathy?
They belong to *you*, after all,
both the crazy cells and the sane ones.
Who are you to differentiate?

The Prowler

Why bolt the doors and lock the windows
of your immunity when he has tools
of entry shaped like parts of your own body?

You remember a few anxious times when you
caught glimpses of him (or her? or neither?)
skulking around shaded edges of your inheritance.

With your first open look at his face,
what if you recognize the earliest friend
of your birth, aeons older than mother and father?

Then it would be out of wonder at his diligent
devotion to you that he takes your breath away.

In Bed Alone

For just a moment or two
I've been allowed to be
only what I am now,

relieved of all thought
of how or why I got here
or where I'm going. And believe

me, this thing that I am
is small, small. A problem
hardly worth sleeping on.

My Two Lives

The life I could have lived,
that other, better one,
is also mine. Who else
can claim it? Each morning, stooping
down, I know that I'm not worthy
to tie my own shoelaces.

The Son of Man

Yes, when taken down, he'd been nailed,
hands and feet, his side pierced, but his
legs were not broken, and how many miles

he has trudged, back and forth around
the earth to torment and redeem
the last twenty centuries of our existence.

A High-Toned Old Christian Gentleman

One detail from the shadowy scene
tells us his posture: his naked toes
are pointing straight up, the soles of his feet
press against nothing more solid than air.
He has for the moment lost his foothold
on the earth where all that happens is real.

And yet he does not go climbing up
the air to heights where grave events
would release his body's weight to all
he could imagine. He is simply
sleeping. His toes twitch with dreams
not in the world but of the world.

Genesis 7:27

"And all the days of Methuselah were nine
hundred sixty and nine years: and
he died."

(This is surely going to great lengths
to show that old age does endanger
your health.)

The Night after Sleep

After the party he idles toward
an hour of reading in his bed
to invite sleep. Prompted by habit

he flicks off lights in kitchen,
dining room, front room, thinking,
"I won't be back this way till morning."

And what an immensely accurate fact
lies secret as a seed in this casual thought
until the miniature dark that sheathes his sleep,

bursts into the one all-containing night
which millions of stars have labored
for millions of years to illuminate.

Games Not to Be Toyed With

Behind Home Plate

This television super-slow-motion
replay shows us the pitcher's fast-ball
floating so lazily toward the batter
we can see the seams revolving.

We can hardly believe the sweat
the pitcher is wiping from his brow,
or the batter's miscalculation in striking
out. It gives us a glimpse of what

it is we measure in clocks and calendars,
how it bulges with both absolute speed
and absolute stillness beyond our knowing.

At Center Court

Backcourt to backcourt
the ball whips flat
across the net by an inch
or ovals over in a top-spin.

Now the players converge
at the net, their racquets
turn animal, the ball leaps off
instincts bared to the quick.

For three hours we've watched
them sweat their bodies to invade,
to defend, one arm lengthened
to sting or caress the air.

At last they are being applauded
into sweaters along the sidelines.
What remains is the stubborn
geometry etched on the same ground

we all walk on. It is still divided
by a wall we can see through
and stretched tighter than nerves,
strung on muscle-frames, can bear

for more than a few hours in the sun.
These rectangles laid down rigid and white
as bones along the packed earth are not now,
are not even a game, are always

a later day, another year, younger bodies.

By Firefly to Tokyo and Back

In July twilight a galaxy
of fireflies twinkles low
across the darkening lawn.

We watch in awe. For them
a labor as inescapable
as the orbiting of stars; for us

silent fireworks celebrating
our patch of earth. They look
like the chirpings of birds we heard

in the half-dark of early dawn.
The distance from birds to fireflies, from ear
to eye, is made from the stuff of lightyears,

but the jetliner winging us to Tokyo
and lighting us back again
only gains or loses sleep.

As always, a matter of dreams.
The belly dancer writhes to her music,
the children go on chanting their games.

Translating the Latin

We were inching our way through *De Senectute*,
a page or half-page at a time. One by one,
in a sequence of our names we never learned to predict,
he called on us to English the Latin we first
had to read aloud. Scanning our scrawls sequestered
in the margins of our page and cribbed from the best
translations we could find, we spoke in the meek
deferential tones befitting our plebeian rank.
("The noblest Roman of them all," our yearbook called
    him.)

Did we ever fool him? We knew that he had heard
our plagiarisms hundreds of times before.
But never once did we guess how deep a game
we all were playing as he listened alike to the worst
and best dissemblers among us. What he heard
must have been that persistent music of old age,
not his, not Cicero's, but ours: a sonata
of the years which only our banal young voices
could compose and which he alone could hear.

How much he could teach us now, trapped inside
our grammar of shrinking sinews! Those suble inflections,
for instance, to fortify our subjunctive or conditional
moods against unwarranted indicative statements;
those periphrastics to guide us safely around
the things we should have learned and forgot;
and those inversions of time which we now surmise,
subjects deferred years after the events of verbs
have commandeered their objects, direct and indirect.

But in surviving we have come to feel almost
at ease with the imperfect syntax of our lives.
We no longer have the will to rememorize
the niceties of our conjugations and declensions.
Besides, he is still ahead of us, some fifty
years beyond old age. What he might teach
us now and in what language we cannot imagine.
All he has left with us is our next assignment,
not telling us when it is due or what it requires.

Evidence

I can't talk to you now,
says the bank robber. Later,
says the killer, I'm in a hurry.
The landlady says, My, my, it's true
they were always going and coming
at all hours but paid their rent on time.

What stays still on the courthouse clock
is the same as what moves round and round
its face. Camera tapes for the evening TV news
revolve, revolve, trying to find a center.
The landlady, it turns out, doesn't know where it is.
The Judge by mistake smashes his watch with his gavel.

Metaporn

Our pornographers have discovered, not
meaning to, that nudity now befits
our tribe as it did at its chilly beginning,
a complete exposure of ourselves before
it's too late to confess; before, that is,
we all have our clothes blown off.

But what an excessive disrobing we've invented,
down to the marrowbones, the soft moist genital
pleasures seared away, leaving exciting positions
of insertion and reception only to be guessed at
from bare skeletal structures. Supposing,

of course, there'll be any leering eyes left
to ogle those pelvic precincts where sons
and daughters found partners, century
after century, to re-enact the naked
bedded antics of their fathers and mothers.

Solitaire Lotto

Suppose, for instance, a someone who
has wagered prayers against so many
years that words and numbers have worn down

to gestures like those of the infant he once
was, blind fragile hands challenging
the empty air. Then, when wakened

by sirens speeding into and out
of earshot, let him cross himself
or merely raise a hand in the dark:

a random quest for at least one other
in dire need somewhere in the world
for whose sake whole cities may be spared.

Natural Relations

Gardening through the Ages

I

A sudden whiff of the spoiled fish
which you forgot to bury
in your garden warns you of
the body you are, or own.

Yesterday when sickling
last year's weeds around
the lilacs, you sliced through the tiny
bones of a bird, still feathered.

Before that, you spaded up
black soil poised between
leaf-shapes and anonymous humus.
It smelled of old secrets unearthed.

II

Eat my body, he said,
given for yours. Then fingered
the loaf into twenty centuries
of crumbs as fine as dust.

Pity the harsh poverty of belief.
The rich young man turns away
in sorrow, the rough fisherman weeps
when the body, come from the tomb

to the seashore, waits to share
with him the broiled fish and to ask
three times, Do you love me?
Then feed them, fisherman, fish them.

And what assurance for Magdalen,
forgiven, but weeping inside
our garden? Do not
touch me, the time is not yet.

Smell of Survival, Long Range

Blood and brain can do nothing with this primitive
scent skimmed off ground soggy with November rain
except to whiff you back to some child of yourself,
maybe to that first slap that tingled you into breathing.

Or farther back? Say, to baby fish, or bird, or reptile
jostled into the pungent savor of an old earth's morning?
Old men learn to forget so much, it may be
they can detect the odor of memory itself.

So wait. Under these dripping leaves of the oak
that grandfather planted, stand still and wait.
Over there from the brambles stirring
at the garden's edge may appear

some weasel-shape with enough cunning
of smell to stay visible among the living.
If nothing be seen, a squeal or squeak may open
your ear to what has long been in the air.

Birds, Chimneys

When we knelt at the cold fireplace to listen
closely, we heard no hint of song, no cheep, no chirp,
only an intermittent flurry of wingtips
against the masonry trying for flying room.
The hoarse whisper of feathers scraped
at a sooty underside of bird-life unknown to us.

A prolonged silence. But when we opened the cast-iron
damper, instead of a dead or half-dead
defeated lump plopping into the ashes
of last night's grate, a live projectile
shot out, as if a rocket launch from our tall
chimney had gone berserk, had backfired
into a crazy zigzag of curves, swerves,
dips and upswings through front room, dining
room, kitchen, study, sunroom, sometimes barely
missing our heads, bouncing off the false promises
of light in windowpanes, but never once resting,
untiring wings determined to translate
our walled-up spaces into outdoor meanings.

At last it found the door we'd been holding
open for it until the whole house was freezing,
and all we had left to do was to look for droppings.
What we found was a trace of soot on one white curtain.

Twenty-two years later on another day
that falls five degrees into the zero of winter
we look out our windowpanes to see
cardinals, doves, juncos, sparrows,
and even a few tough, scornful jays
warming themselves on the rims of our neighbors'
chimneys. As they huddle there, fidgeting,
adjusting their feathers, they warm us too,
just as they are, just as we are.

Winter Holiday in Sunshine City

This indolent wind fondling
the fronds of palm trees chafes
the conscience of my northern skin.
I detect a warning in the wanton
pleasure that tingles up
to me from bay waters mouthing
and tonguing the naked beaches.

In a sudden fantasy as savage
as hunger, I am lugging my body
through white drifts, my own warm meat,
heavily wrapped, steaming
from nostrils in a frigid wind.

Is there a touch of grace
the blood needs in having to learn,
one season each year, that time
is driving toward absolute zero?
If so, what a pity, after
so many winters, to miss
even one such fragile favor.

Mid-Winter Greetings

Dismiss the wide gray face
of sky; it expresses nothing,
is almost absent.

Stray flakes of white
meander down, so few
you could count them.

Starlings in a dark cloud
drift into black branches
of a distant treetop and become
so still they can't be seen.

Dead leaves left hanging
in the nearby oak quiver
in a breeze as brief,
as inconclusive as a sigh,
then are dead again.

The snow of last week's
blizzard lies flat
on its back. Its rigor
tightens the arctic cold.

There's barely movement
enough to keep time
alive, the faint tempo
of waiting for nothing
that can be spoken.

A postcard picture of winter
Lotus-land. It tells you
that peace is infinitely
desirable, that only
the dead can endure it.

Mountain

To have a mountain you need a lot of room.
Also a solid base because a mountain is heavy.
And you should have some sky to spare
because a mountain hoists itself up
into a permanent snowy season taller
than July, disturbing your horizon.

Though you might spend your life here,
to presume you could domesticate a mountain
would be like pretending you kept a dinosaur
penned up in your backyard as a pet.

However, from a proper distance you can
sometimes gaze and gaze at a mountain
until you feel yourself leaning upon
its craggy, primitive hide as if at home
in its long resistance to earthly weather.

And a mountain makes it hard to be
afraid the world might disappear
while you are being still and merely looking.

INTERROGATION

You watched the alleged
disappearance of the sun
which people call sunset?

Yes.

Where were you at the time?

I can only say I was
where I continued to be.

What do you mean?

I mean I know I was not
where that tall pine was,
a short distance away, because
I saw it vanish into total darkness.

How did it happen?

Like the rest of the landscape
it faded without a sound.

But you felt the wind brushing past you?

Yes.

Do you think the wind
was implicated in the loss of light?

It wasn't strong enough.
It touched me gently, cool
and refreshing after the hot day.

You've mentioned the faint
but incessant barking
of a dog in the distance.

Yes.

Did it sound to you
like a warning? Or perhaps
a prophecy fulfilled?

I think the dog was barking
for private canine reasons.

You've said the birds fell silent.
Were they concealing things
we ought to know? Would you
suspect them of complicity?

No. They tuck their heads
under their wings only
to secure their own bird-dreams.

Where were the birds hiding?

I don't believe they were hiding.
They were nestling in the trees for sleep.

Did you see them there?

No.

Then how do you know?

I don't.

Quandary

When you push the emptied dishwasher
back from the sink to its resting place,
its wheels don't squeal as usual. And through
the open window comes a cool
breeze, a parting, patronizing
caress from the torrid afternoon.
Yet your day does not close whole. You recall

how quarks of all colors, all nuclear spins
and forces combine to query, as if
they are quibbles, the very questions you strain
to raise at your utmost stretch of mind.
Should you, then, look for unexamined
quirks in your bundles of nerves, or for
unexpected wobbles in the light from stars?

The Twister That Missed Us

A flash of thunder has stunned our electric
clock on the kitchen wall. At dawn
it circles astray in a vanished night.
Once losing the scent of our fugitive hours
this pointer we trained finds only us.

Do lightning-propelled wind and rain
have a father? There must be a family
language which they obey, gibberish
to us, but for them as clear as touch.

Huddled in basements candle-lighted
like catacombs, what was left
for us to pray to except the ring
of stillness riding at peace in the storm's eye?

Incident in a Rain of Violence

For a man about to be struck
by lightning the broad sky
is no different from a dark alley
where a pistol takes aim at him.

Experts in the law will find
this fatality "an act of God"
with no blame attached.

Astronomy

It would seem that loaded
with the debris of suffering
accumulated from the centuries

of our history the earth
might become too heavy
to spin accurately around

its axis. The quite recent ovens
of death-camp crematoriums,
embracing the flames of Hiroshima,

ought to be enough to clog
the earth's smooth parabola
around the all-seeing sun.

And yet according to our own
meticulous scrutiny our planet
continues to perform like clockwork.

It must be that in the breathless
lofty spaces through which
it moves, its burden of human

misery becomes weightless.

A Late Twentieth-Century Prayer

We've been taught for two thousand years
that not a single sparrow can fall
outside your notice. And now
you've given us leave to perfect

microscopic spectacles insightful enough
to show us your meticulous concern
with these minute particles in the body
of the world we inhabit, so alien to our everyday

perception we know them only by their nicknames,
some of them snuffed out in fractions of a second.
You must have, then, some inclination
to attend to all my little kind and me,

orphaned on earth, this tiny cinder flung
helplessly around and around
a helplessly burning star. We trust your interest
in us may be what locally we call love.

Family Relations

TRICYCLE

Behind the frisking, farting tail
of our young mare, Nellie, we were riding
the seven-mile stretch of dirt road
from the "burg" back home to our village.

Wedged between my knees was the tricycle,
hatched at last, shiny-real, from the page
which I had kept warm all winter long
in the Sears and Roebuck catalogue.

My father was slapping the reins against
Nellie's rump, and when the hurried
wheels bounced in and out of the caked-mud
ruts, he would yell, Watch out! There it goes
over the side! And I would grab
the handlebars and hang on hard.
My mother said, Will, stop teasing
the child like that. But what did she know.

The enormous sunlight of that whole summer
held still and firm, I thought, all around me
while I pedaled my three wheels up
and down our brick sidewalks so fast I saw
the spokes spin into one flashing blur.

Even so, I could fly no faster than the Twentieth
Century Limited which I was driving
at full-throttle, whistling my mile-a-minute
disdain at boy-size towns like ours.

Yet I was straining toward that orgasmic
peak in time where speed explodes
in a tower of fire, and beginnings and ends
of rails and sidewalks melt into one moment.

My own children were clinging to my back
like laboratory monkeys. They stared
ahead in terror at speed as pure
as instant sunlight, knowing they could not
let go of their primitive father-flesh.

Incident in a Long Story

Gathering from her clotheslines the billowing
bundles of her half-dry Monday wash
into her arms, my mother shouted to me
to rescue my tricycle on the wooden walk.

I got astraddle of the metal frame
just in time to scream with the thrill
that exploded through it, a close echo
of the lightning bolt that scarred
forever the trunk of our neighbor's great elm.

In that split-second I learned I wanted
to live, one flash bright enough for a lifetime.
As if God had said with destructive emphasis:
I tell you what I told myself at the start,
that all that I have made is good.

Watching the Nightly TV News

I feel for my belly button.
It is still intact, firmly knotted.
There's no escape; I've been born,
no matter how many decades ago
my father and my mother died.

Recent Family History

Looking out at us from their photographs,
mothers and fathers, aunts and uncles,
now dead for forty-five years or more,
don't recognize us, can't even imagine us.

And we are helpless to penetrate the safety
of their innocence, leaving us to become
this alien, diminished species, Treblinka
having taught us that to be alive can be

a capital crime and Hiroshima showing us
how most efficiently to execute the criminals.

Love Song in a Minor Key

It's not this harmony of naked
bodies clasped together, the moist
blood-swelled thrust fitted
into blood-swelled orifice.

What perfects their night of love
is something they know they both fit into,
like the ancient dark that drifts in
over them from the open window.

It's something they were born with
but can't possess. As if each one
had mortally wounded the other
near the beginning of time,

and now they've found in this duet
of such bodies as are left to them
a way to claim the sweetness
of their hurt if not its healing.

Eileen and the Daylilies

I wonder how my glance, hardened
by years of falling on rows of brick
and stone buildings, on metallic lines
of traffic, when falling casually
on her, melts into air which I must
breathe into me every moment to stay alive,

and how the air darkening in my veins
must be driven through my heart and breath
to be restored so that I can see her
in our garden, all new, as she fingers
those gracefully curved blades of sunlight,
the lilies that will live for one whole day.

Her Wealth of Shells

Back home again in her heartland she's picked out her best.
She arranges them on a sidetable like a showcase of jewels.

She remembers the night she wakened to the bay water
shaking the air, its whole body a froth of whitecaps,
its bare fangs tearing at the sand and the seawall.

The next morning it wallowed in a bath
of sunshine. Its mammoth weight,
lolling about, lifted a gentle overflow
of ripples along the shore. And then

as if this salt-water monster had casually
tossed it to her, there at her feet
in the wet sand lay the prize
she'd been looking for for weeks —
a King's Crown, perfect in every detail.

How could such a clumsy, amorphous
giant teach its little soft ones
to spin from their gelatin bodies these exquisite
private castles, hard as stone?

Now they are here, spread out before her:
ribbed, whorled, voluted, turreted,
in patterns artfully imprecise,
striated or speckled with bands and dabs
of color, smooth as polished gems,
or pebbled with whims of warts and pockmarks.

Granted, the elemental need to survive,
but why this excess, what need to be beautiful?
She tries to imagine how much her forebears
had to forget, aeons ago, while learning
to make her human. One by one

she fingers the shells with names she has had
to learn, like a child, from picture books:
cockle, pecten, whelk, coquina, tellin.
Those with punning nicknames sound
closest to her: tulip, cat's paw,
cat's eye, auger, worm shell, olive.

She watches the landlocked light wither
to mere husks the fabled treasure
she meant to bring home in her plastic bag,

yet says amen to the space that has been given
her in air, on dry land, where she has room
to love them if not to know them. She picks up
her King's Crown. The sultry midwestern
afternoon sweats salt in her hand.

For Eileen on Her Birthday: Walking with Her Around Saint Joseph's Lake

She drives the car but when we park,
she hands me the keys to carry.
Before I can knock out my pipe
she has crossed the paved road
and stands ready like a traffic cop
to signal me a safe moment to join her.
Then she bounds down the concrete steps
as if she's going to hunt something
we can bring home to eat for dinner.

We stand together on the path that will
revolve us around Saint Joseph's lake.
She announces our starting time.
Although her watch is faster than mine,
I say nothing. For a few paces
we exchange banalities about weather
and temperature, and then she is off,
soon ten yards ahead. After we have rounded
the boathouse curve of the path and are
coming to the weeping willows
I run to catch up to her and make
some hard-breathing comments
about the patterns of shallow waves
woven in the water and the nuances
of cloud-colors reflected on the dome
and spire on the other side.

She has already observed them
and maybe dismissed them.
She begins to talk about details
of foliage and flowers along the path
that I haven't seen. I lag behind.

By the time we get to what is left
of the woods I wonder if the joggers
who pass and meet us know we are walking
together. They greet us separately.
Maybe they think I am chasing her.

I am. At the tall colonnade
of walnut trees she is out of sight,
until I see her sitting on the steps,
waiting. "Although, looking back,
I couldn't see you," she says, "you're only
three minutes late." Space and time.

I think back to my many years
of illusion: me sitting still
through long hours but striding
through thoughts and images
of muscular language builders
of books while she lay sleeping.
The race between tortoise and hare,
but when Saint Joseph of the Lake
tells the fable, which is which?

Last night, calling from Los Angeles,
our daughter asked me, "Did you ever
think you'd be married to a sixty-eight-
year-old woman?" But our daughter
was inside our marriage for only nine months.
I try to think from the outside, like her question.
But it's beside any point I can make.
Instead, I try to think, What if
her mother had never been born? I can't.

In the innocent parabola of the path
around Joseph's lake there must be hidden
some mechanism that betrays little
but means everything. Like a clumsy
geared wheel meshed with intricate
accuracy into a smaller, faster one,
for no reason, except that it works.

I try to imagine myself circling
the lake alone at my own pace,
greeting the joggers with a nod,
but never geared to anyone at all.
I can see only incalculable disasters,
like suddenly, in mid-stride, forgetting
how to walk, or plodding around
and around in a void with no one
sitting on the concrete steps
to tell me when and where to stop.

DAUGHTER DEPARTING, ARRIVING

She's nearing the narrow canvas tunnel that opens
into her flight. Her hand and our hands
winging farewells from above our heads, have already
signaled the rift between airborne and earthbound.

She disappears inside, leaving us only
this whimsical shadow of herself, a giant
facsimile of a bird sprawled on the tarmac.

We must wait, it seems, for minute
after minute to mount a montage of glimpses
at all her twenty-nine years before this stiff-winged
monster consents to lumber sullenly into place
on the takeoff runway, diesels faintly hissing.

Here too we're compelled to linger, to be taught again
how tedious suspense can be, as if our nerves,
though aging, could forget the growing gravity
of the nine months that weaned her out of hiding.

And now, abruptly interrupting all time past,
blind turbines, trained by touch with the runway,
are assaulting our common air, demanding flight.

(Isn't this fabricated promise to lift
her human weight above the clouds too *loud?*)

But with only a few heartbeats of pavement
left, the air complies with an upsurge
in our lungs like a newly invented way of breathing.

And this gawky, contrived creature rises
into as lovely a bird or angel as poet
or mystic ever conceived. Then dwindles
to erase the vanishing point of our scene.

Why have we stayed on for this still, invisible
moment, if not to listen again for her first
birth-cry and from there to follow her
through our everyday habit of breath and pulse
to the very brink of the heavens and (who knows?) beyond.

We turn from an empty sky
to face each other. A quick laugh
confesses we've both been caught
indulging in the substance of things half-seen.

Our mutual guilt links us helplessly
together. Arm in arm we leave for the parking
lot, then home. But what is home until,
two hours later, the telephone rings?

She is down to earth again, tired and hungry.
We barely have time to ask, How was your flight?
Bumpy, she says, from Dayton on, but the landing was perfect.

What Can "Grand" Mean?

Here is grandfather with his granddaughter
on his lap. They are reading aloud, sometimes
in unison, more often taking turns,
from a child's alphabet book, big and small
letters repeated in pictures and words.

Back to his ABC's grandfather
is old enough to know he is where
he belongs, just now beginning to learn
the rudimentary but difficult lesson
that he was born to die. He's surprised

how easily from the same gaunt letters
he can teach a child warm in his arms
that she was born only to live.

Should the daughter-mother suddenly
come upon them now, in the folds
of the overstuffed chair, she might wonder
if she had caught them in a pre-creation
scandal, nestled together in one womb.

Fellow Travelers

Time and Again

Young men and women
visit us, their eyes, their faces
fresh with life as it is now.

They bring us the glad news
that we've been allowed
to live for a while with them
in their unknown future.

Resistance

When your eyes begin to blur
the lively distinctions of color
and shape in the things around you,

as if complaining, Haven't we seen
enough? And your ears, weary
and bored, neglect the finer

modulations of meaningful
sound in speech and song;
and your feet move reluctantly,

even for short distances, heavy
with many trivial and futile
destinations, you must

not acquiesce. You must
resist, not to retrieve
yourself but to rescue the young

who wish with the same passion
you once were filled with, to live
as long as you have and longer.

Oldest Guest at the Celebration

These youngsters in their thirties, forties and fifties
are no longer amateurs of life, but the luck
of living still shines in their eyes with such
easy intensity it warms you to be
crowded among them. As they talk with you

you hear their words blend into songs
you recognize as from a distance.
Do they echo old neighborhoods
where you have lived, or the unknown place
before you? Or both? It may mean only
that you are becoming slightly deaf.

What does it matter? You are here.
Drink your wine and listen. Enjoy the party.

Injunction to the Young

Don't abandon your elders
(already weak with age)
to their burden of inherited

ignorance. Jaded as they are
with the luminous discoveries
of their youth now fading into

clichés, they are as vulnerable
to new knowledge as kindergarten
children and are as easily

enlightened or deceived.

Gerontocrats

We wear our years like a badge
that envelopes us from head
to foot, recognized everywhere —

thinning white hair, wrinkled
face, sagging shoulders, slow
cautious gait. What it

conceals is that our selective
order is by nature
compelled to induct all
who live too long to protest.